BOOK PREVIEW

What is the original intent of the almighty God's heart? Wouldn't He desire for the beings, made in His image and likeness, to function accordingly? We are created to abide in a harmonious relationship with Him. How could this omnipotent, omniscient, omnipresent, all-wise creator require anything of His creation while keeping us in the dark?

The first act of His sovereignty we are privy to is rebuking darkness. This helps us to understand His desire to reveal Himself and enlighten us to His ways. Can a true fellowship be established and respected if those involved are not open and honest?

My earnest desire is that readers would find probable cause to reexamine the facts currently held as "foundational truth" and see if they align themselves with what they will be challenged to understand. God's desire is for His children get off the emotional rollercoaster and onto the path of faith that we've been prescribed to walk. Even as the journey is just as important as the destination, the direction of the journey determines the destination.

The SUBSTANCE of FAITH

J. ALAN TIMMS

WestBow
PRESS®
A DIVISION OF THOMAS NELSON
& ZONDERVAN

Copyright © 2024 J. Alan Timms.

All rights reserved. No part of this book may be used or reproduced by any means, graphic, electronic, or mechanical, including photocopying, recording, taping or by any information storage retrieval system without the written permission of the author except in the case of brief quotations embodied in critical articles and reviews.

This book is a work of non-fiction. Unless otherwise noted, the author and the publisher make no explicit guarantees as to the accuracy of the information contained in this book and in some cases, names of people and places have been altered to protect their privacy.

WestBow Press books may be ordered through booksellers or by contacting:

WestBow Press
A Division of Thomas Nelson & Zondervan
1663 Liberty Drive
Bloomington, IN 47403
www.westbowpress.com
844-714-3454

Because of the dynamic nature of the Internet, any web addresses or links contained in this book may have changed since publication and may no longer be valid. The views expressed in this work are solely those of the author and do not necessarily reflect the views of the publisher, and the publisher hereby disclaims any responsibility for them.

Any people depicted in stock imagery provided by Getty Images are models, and such images are being used for illustrative purposes only. Certain stock imagery © Getty Images.

Scripture quotations are taken from the Holy Bible, King James Version.

ISBN: 979-8-3850-3066-8 (sc)
ISBN: 979-8-3850-3067-5 (hc)
ISBN: 979-8-3850-3068-2 (e)

Library of Congress Control Number: 2024916217

Print information available on the last page.

WestBow Press rev. date: 10/24/2024

Dedication

To the most high sovereign God (יהוה), the creator of the universe, and to His beloved Son the Lord Yashua (יהשצ) our Redeemer.

To my wife Anita and our kids for their support. To Rabbi Tzuriel Mann, whose love and dedication to the Word of God inspired me to search for the deeper things of God and not settle for mediocrity.

Contents

Dedication v
Introduction ix

Chapter 1	The Breath of God 1
Chapter 2	God is Love 13
Chapter 3	Mercy: The Extension of Love 25
Chapter 4	Grace: God's Empowerment 37
Chapter 5	Redemption: God's Legal Loophole 45
Chapter 6	Reconciliation: Covenant Balance 53
Chapter 7	Restoration: Welcome Back 61
Chapter 8	Justification: Divine Alignment 71
Chapter 9	Atonement: The Ultimate Connection ...79
Chapter 10	All Things Work Together.....................89

Afterword..97

Introduction

When God laid the foundation of the universe, he infused it with keys to unlock doors and reveal truths that would validate His existence. In doing so, He would expose the depth of His love for humanity. The master key is faith and its composition. The Word of God declares, "Faith is the *substance* of things hoped for, the evidence of things not seen" (Heb. 11:1; emphasis added). What is the substance that scripture declares to us? What is the composition of our hope?

It is imperative that the word *foundation* is emphasized. Scripture says that God's works were established or finished before (Eph. 1:4) and since (Heb. 4:3; Rev. 13:8) the foundation of the world. The foundation establishes the purpose of our relationships and walks with God (Matt. 7:24–27). It would behoove the Bible student, as well as one seeking truth, to investigate from this viewpoint.

What is the original intent of the almighty God's heart? Wouldn't He desire for the beings, made in His image and likeness, to function accordingly? We are created to abide in a harmonious relationship with Him. How could this omnipotent, omniscient, omnipresent, all-wise creator require anything of His creation while keeping us in the dark?

The first act of His sovereignty we are privy to is rebuking darkness. This helps us to understand His desire to reveal Himself and enlighten us to His ways. Can a true fellowship be established and respected if those involved are not open and honest?

My earnest desire is that the reader would find probable cause to reexamine the facts currently held as "foundational truth" and see if they align themselves with what he or she will be challenged to understand. It is God's desire for His children get off the emotional rollercoaster and onto the path of faith that we've been prescribed to walk. Even as the journey is just as important as the destination, the direction of the journey determines the destination.

When the word *faith* is used, it must, in the heart of the believer in Christ, carry a specific and deliberate connotation. I am of the deepest conviction that there is only one true God and the term *faith* belongs to Him only. We must remember that even He has declared to us through His word that there is "One Lord, *one faith*, one baptism" (Eph. 4:5; emphasis added). The adversary is the master of the counterfeit. Various religious entities use the term *faith* while claiming to self-validate their spirituality. We must know that faith is relational and not just spiritual. It would also pay to note that these other entities make no claim to have a god that answers prayer and communicates and communes with His children. They claim to be followers, or disciples if you will, but not children.

It is my earnest desire and prayer that the body of Christ enter a dimension of truth that will foster unity and love toward our God and one another. John 13:35 states, "By this shall all men know that ye are my disciples, if ye have love one to another." Ephesians 4:3 states that we should be "endeavoring to keep the unity of the Spirit in the bond of peace."

1
THE BREATH OF GOD

When we speak on the issue of faith, we must begin at its source to apprehend its function and capability. The Bible student must always, with great care, concern himself or herself with the origin of a matter. When we examine the nature of Elohim, we must begin with the fact that He is Spirit. Please note that I didn't say a spirit. He should not be spoken of in a manner to suggest He is equal to any other spirit being. He is the source of all Spirit as well as all things natural.

From this, we are forced to draw certain conclusions on how He functions, communicates, and interacts with His creation. The canon of scripture in Genesis 1:1–3 reveals that after assessing the darkness and positioning Himself accordingly, He spoke. His manner of speaking was intentional in addressing the desired result or solution concerning the darkness. He said, "Let there be light" (Gen. 1:3).

From this point, it becomes necessary, since we are discussing faith, to state that scripture reveals that "through faith we understand that the worlds (ages) were *framed* by the word of God, so that things which are seen were not made of things which do appear" (Heb. 11:3; emphasis added). The power of Elohim released through His word caused all that He foreordained in structuring creation to manifest. By His word alone the material realm manifests from the immaterial. The aforementioned scripture shows that faith is infused with the word of God. Thus, we confirm that "In the beginning was the Word, and the Word was with God, and the *Word was God*" (John 1:1; emphasis added). As Romans 10:17 states, "So then, faith cometh by hearing, and hearing by the word of God." Having established that faith is released or activated when the word of God is spoken, let us proceed to examine the first scenario in which we see faith on exhibit.

In Genesis 1:2, we find that darkness was the issue upon which the almighty Creator focused His attention. Remembering that Elohim is Spirit; this darkness had to represent more than physical obscurity. After all, if it was physical in nature only, He could have merely positioned the luminaries manifested in verses 14 through 15. Yet He called the instrument of rebuke "light." Why? I believe to fully understand, we should examine the components or substance of the darkness as it relates to the original Hebrew text.

Genesis 1:2 states, "And the earth was without form, and void; and *darkness* was upon the face of the deep. And the Spirit of God *moved* upon the face of the waters" (emphasis added). The word *darkness* is the Hebrew word *choshek* (kho-shek). While it carries in the literal sense the connotation of physical darkness, it also has applications that make it relevant to Elohim's plan of redemption. These applications are misery, *death*, destruction, ignorance, sorrow, wickedness and obscurity. These are all things that our all-wise, sovereign Creator rebuked in order that His mercy should prevail on our behalf. Please note that death is one of the components conquered from the foundation of the world. In His wisdom, He created a legal loophole to deliver us from the wages of sin.

If it is necessary to examine the darkness, it is likewise necessary to examine the light. Before we can proceed, we must consider the placement of God's Spirit before the light was summoned. The word *moved,* as seen in the text, is the Hebrew word *rachaph* (raw-khaf), which means "to brood" or "to hover." It also has a very distinct word picture association. This word picture is one of someone (Elohim) looking directly over a situation. Now this word picture reveals the course of events. It tells us that Elohim rebuked the darkness by looking at it in a confrontational manner and speaking the solution. In addition, note that His purpose for rebuking the darkness was to reveal the Creator to the creation and become the foundation of creation. In this revelation, He shows Himself as light. The beauty of light as we see it in the physical realm is that it is multifaceted. It takes a prism to break it down so one can see its composition. That is the purpose of this literary work. Just as Elohim's Word comes to us in the form of the Bible, the Holy Spirit serves as a prism to give us clarity and revelation. The totality of the matter is that Elohim desired a relationship with His creation that was without obstruction. Now we understand that this light is the revelation of Himself. The creation must have a revelation of the Creator to know what it is to be and how it is to function. He is the true Source, and for the creation to have *re*source, it must receive from Him.

FAITH AS A FRAMER

The word of God declares that "through faith we understand that the worlds (ages) were *framed* by the word of God" (Heb. 11:3; emphasis added). The periods of time, which we like to refer to as dispensations, were structured by the wisdom of God's word. We must note that time is an instrument of structure. Yet, it remains subservient in its relationship to eternity and thus does not restrict the operation of faith. Only as an instrument of structure does it serve to reveal God's event markers. To further this conclusion, we must examine a word that the Father positions in the beginning of scripture. That word is found in Genesis 1:14, and it is the word *seasons*. The Word declares, "And God said, 'Let there be lights in the firmament of the heaven to divide the day from the night; and let them be for signs, and for *seasons*, and for days, and for years" (emphasis added). This particular word is the Hebrew word *moedim*, which translates as "appointed times." This helps us to understand that everything Elohim does is intentional, purposeful, and precise. Job mentions that "all the days of my appointed time will I wait, till my change come" (). He had a revelation into the seasons of God. As seasons change in the natural, likewise they also change in God's economy and in our functional alignment. These prescribed changes are appointed by the order of Elohim.

What was appropriate in the winter season is not compatible for the summer. The writer of Ecclesiastes states, "To everything there is a season, and a time to every purpose under the heaven" (Eccl. 3:1). The Lord Himself states in Genesis 8:22, "While the earth remaineth, seedtime and harvest, cold and heat, and summer and winter, and day and night shall not cease."

Please note that the Father starts with times and seasons and then progresses to chronology, as He did in Genesis 1:14. This is a clear indicator that He would have us understand and be concerned with how He has structured His economy. If anyone should know what the Lord is doing or has prescribed for a particular season, it is the body of Christ. One of the children of Israel's greatest character flaws was they failed to acknowledge the pattern and blueprint provided exclusively for them to reveal this wisdom from God.

In the wilderness, they were given God's prophet Moses, the tabernacle, and the law. The prophet spoke concerning the heart of God. The tabernacle provided not only a place of worship, but also held the revelation of God's love, the timetable of God's economy, and the relationship between heaven and earth. The law was the social construct that, when followed, would foster unity, sanctify them as a nation, and secure the presence and the favor of almighty God. They had everything needed to govern the issues of life.

We, as believers in the Lord Jesus Christ, have a very serious indictment against us. We have been given the gift of the Holy Spirit and have the volume of the Bible to reference. We have all they had and more and yet refuse to allow the ministry of the Holy Spirit to sanctify us as a holy nation and a royal priesthood.

Allow me to reference a passage of scripture that speaks to God's desire in sanctifying a people who are called unto Him and by His Name. Deuteronomy 4:5–7 states,

"Behold I have taught you statutes and judgments, even as the Lord my God commanded me, that ye should do in the land whither ye go to possess it. Keep therefore and do them; for this is your wisdom and understanding in the sight of the nations, which shall hear all these statutes, and say, 'Surely this great nation is a wise and understanding people.' For what nation is there so great, who hath God so nigh unto them, as the Lord our God is in all things that we call upon him for? And what nation is there so great, that has statutes and judgments so righteous as all this law, which I set before you this day?"

When I embrace the purpose for God's social construct, I understand, by reason of principle, that to fulfill the law of God's love ensures the fullness of the finished work of Christ. When I speak of the finished work of Christ, I am referring to such things as redemption, restoration, reconciliation, and so forth. We are the redeemed of the Lord (Ps. 107:2), but have we allowed faith to redeem all that the Father predestined for us to receive as an inheritance? We have been restored to a right relationship with the Father (Ps. 23:3), but have we allowed the Father to restore all that is to be inherited by our bloodlines? We have been reconciled unto God (2 Cor. 5:18), but have we allowed the Father to reconcile all the issues of our hearts? These are just a few of the tenets of our faith we are supposed to fulfil in our walks with God (Phil. 2:12–13). These tenets, and others that will be outlined in the chapters to come, serve as major factors in our sanctification as the body of Christ.

As I lay these foundational principles, I pray the reader will conceptualize a more holistic dynamic of our salvation. The exhale of almighty God has secured us a living hope that consists of "exceeding great and precious promises whereby we are partakers of the divine nature" (2 Pet. 1:4). As we see the day of the Lord's return approaching, we can no longer afford to marginalize our responsibility to manifest the glory of our Father and His kingdom.

As it further relates to the framework of God's economy, there is an alignment that relates to His appointed times, designed to guide us in a way that provides foresight about what is next on God's calendar. Allow me to share this example from scripture. The magi who traveled from the east (Asia) told Herod they saw a sign in the heavens, alerting them of the time and general location of "He who is born King of the Jews" (). God did say that the heavenly luminaries would serve as "signs and for *seasons"* (moedim). It is historically understood that through the Talmud, they were able to decipher the language and know what sign would reveal this season. What I find fascinating is that the season was revealed to them about the time the angel spoke to Mary. Their journey was believed to take approximately two years. This implies that their study and revelation of the scripture provided insight into God's economy while also revealing the surety of their expectation. Who would travel for two years to present gifts of worship if they were unsure of what God had ordained? This is the power of prophecy. This is how the body of Christ is supposed to function.

Please allow me to state that the magi's use of the stars in no way supports what the world knows as astrology or the zodiac. That is a product of humankind's fallen nature and is perverted from its natural purpose. God has structured everything through faith. We need to understand and embrace that faith gives us the surety of the finished work of God. Even as Christ Jesus declared on the cross, "It is finished," let us move forward into the assurance of what God has completed in Christ for us.

2
GOD IS LOVE

> Beloved, let us love one another: for love is of God; and every one that loveth is born of God, and knoweth God. *He that loveth not knoweth not God; for God is love.*
> —1 JOHN 4:7–8 (EMPHASIS ADDED)

*A*s we begin to explore the tenets of our faith, it serves us well to begin with who God is. He is the foundation of all things holy and righteous. When we as believers speak about love, it behooves us to remember that the origin of love is God.

We must examine this issue not only through scripture, but also by contrast. That contrast is the human idea of love verses the reality of God's love. When most people speak on the issue of love, they equate it to be, or connect it to, an expression of human emotion. Although love, as we know it, can foster emotion, it is in God's arena of operation, so much more.

As I look at the human experience of love, it presents itself as an intellectual and emotional bond developed over time through the expression and sharing of common interests. These common interests need to be more than types of foods, music, or favorite vacation spots. Although those interests will come in handy, the most important is what each person sees in the future.

If people would take time to befriend each other and express their visions and future goals, they would be able to discern if they could arrive there together or maintain a relationship that would foster respect as they travel different paths. Sadly, in some instances, the intellectual aspect is omitted and those involved are left with a shallow experience that will lead to an unhealthy "soul tie" and leave the relationship greatly lacking. I believe this is a major reason that the divorce rate in this country (United States) is so high. People don't take time to examine what it takes to form a true relationship based on honesty, respect, and genuine concern for the other person's well-being and prosperity. Please note that when the truth is not known, a misconception will fill its void. Relationship was designed by the almighty Creator to holistically enhance those involved. Regardless of the dynamic, whether it is husband and wife, siblings, or friends, we should bring growth and enhancement to the relationship. The depletion of our society's moral, ethical, and economic fiber results from not knowing and understanding what God's original blueprint for relationship is. This blueprint is called covenant.

Covenant is the means by which God established relationship and it is the *only* relationship He acknowledges. You may see people prospering because they employ certain principles that God has ordained in order to prosper. That does not mean that they are in covenant relationship with Him. Through covenant, we should receive the revelation of His being and love toward us. Remember, God *is* love. God's expression of love has always been, and always will be, experienced in demonstration. To grasp this truth, one only need understand the concept of deity and the power of God. The Bible's account of creation provides a beautiful picture of this love. Through this account, we observe God create and structure the heavens and the earth and then place it under human stewardship. What an awesome act of benevolence! He could have chosen not to create and would have remained just as awesome as He always has been. Yet, he chose to create and bring humankind into a cooperative juncture for its care. Simply put, everything He did was to the benefit of humankind, the pinnacle of His creation.

Our all-wise Creator expressed His desire for us when He said, "Let them have dominion" (Gen. 1:26). With that desire, He also incorporated an empowerment to achieve the desired result. This empowerment is called *grace* and will be explored in a later chapter.

To further contrast the love of God against the human idea of love, we need to look at the cooperation of all other tenets at work in the crucifixion of our Lord

Jesus Christ. These also will be discussed in forthcoming chapters. The Apostle John wrote, "For God so love the *world,* that he gave his only begotten Son, that whosoever believeth in him should not perish, but have everlasting life" (). The reason I emphasized the word *world* in that passage is because of its translation. As found in the Greek text, it could be rendered as *order,* from the word *cosmos.* Thus, John writes, "for God so loved his order that he gave his one and only Son" (). God was so committed to the *restoration* of His order (humankind's dominion) that the price of *redemption* was his only begotten Son, Jesus, the Christ. This is *atonement* in demonstration. Here is God *reconciling* all things unto himself through Christ Jesus. Through this act, His blood was shed to be presented on the true *mercy* seat in heaven and *grace* can now be imputed unto all who by faith believe.

The elders of my younger days had a saying: "Love is what it does." They understood that love is not in what you say but what you do. The Lord Jesus said, "Greater love hath no man than this, that a man lay down his life for his friends" (Jn. 15:13). You see, it's what one does for the betterment of another or others that establishes the presence of love. It is so much more than an emotion, yet it will provoke a passion for the cause to be served. As revealed by scripture, we understand that God's concept of love is not only benevolent, it is also self-sacrificing. This is how important it is for God to maintain His integrity. He does not and cannot change from what He originally established through his word. Again, God will not compromise His integrity. Numbers 23:19 states, "God is not a man that he should lie; neither the son of man that he should repent: hath he said, and shall he not do it? Or hath he spoken, and shall he not make it good?" Not only is His love self-sacrificing and benevolent, but it is also steadfast or unchanging.

Another thing to consider is how God's love is infused with His wisdom. He is able to bring His will to pass regardless of any resistance or rebellion by the powers that be. Psalm 2 gives great insight into this facet of truth. This psalm reveals that there comes a day in which humanity's leaders take counsel against the Lord, and against His anointed. They conspire to establish autonomy from the Lord's rule, but the scripture states, "He that sitteth in the heavens shall laugh: the Lord shall have them in derision" (verse 4). Another scripture that supports this is Isaiah 14:27, which declares, "For the Lord of hosts hath purposed, and who shall disannul it? And his hand is stretched out, and who shall turn it back?" We must embrace that what God has predetermined cannot be halted by the counsel of humans. Nothing can override His sovereignty. This is extremely important since He has included you in the scheme He has ordained. You were always a part of His master plan and ordained to be a beneficiary of His will. For this reason, the Apostle Paul wrote to the church at Rome,

> For I am persuaded, that neither death, nor life, nor angels, nor principalities, nor powers, nor things present, nor things to come, 'Nor height, nor depth, nor any other creature, shall be able to separate us from the love of God, which is in Christ Jesus our Lord. (Rom. 8:38–39)

If you persevere, God's love will prevail on your behalf. Remember this also: "For the eyes of the Lord run to and fro throughout the whole earth, to show himself strong in the behalf of them whose heart is perfect toward him" (2 Chron. 16:9a).

In continuing to contrast the concept of God's love with the ideas of fallen humanity, it would profit us to observe the behavior of the unregenerate to see if it aligns itself with the description that scripture provides in 1 Corinthians 13.

I find it interesting how people can profess to love someone, perhaps a family member or a spouse or maybe even someone who has been a close associate for a number of years. Yet, when a situation arises that fosters conflict, people are more likely express anger rather than a desire for reconciliation. Most of us have heard, if only in the news, about couples whose relationship turns violent or deadly. What happened to the love that was supposed be there? The word of God declares that love does not behave rudely, does not seek its own benefit, is not easily provoked, and does not think to do evil (1 Cor. 13:5). Siblings have disputes and don't speak to each other for years, or ever again. I contend that these things happen because fallen humanity does know God's guidelines for love. As long as people try to facilitate love through emotions, the rollercoaster ride will never end. Emotions or feelings, for various reasons, change. Until humanity can reasonably conclude this is true, we will never seek the higher truth of God's wisdom.

Again, I must state that love is passionate for the cause to be served. The first chapter of the book of Acts reveals to us that Christ showed Himself alive to many after His passion. What was His passion? The crucifixion by which He shed His blood for our redemption. The Bible also declares no one would consider making such a sacrifice except if the reward outweighed the suffering. Again, scripture declares that to understand the magnitude of Christ's passion, we should be "looking unto Jesus the author and finisher of our faith; *who for the joy that was set before him endured the cross, despising the shame, and is set down at the right hand of the throne of God"* (Heb. 12:2; emphasis added). It is obvious that the reward outweighs the suffering. Anytime that someone becomes passionate for a cause, especially the cause of Christ, there will be opposition, persecution, and misunderstanding. Yet, that does not deter because the love of God is fueling the passion to accomplish the objective and finish the course.

Another reason that passion drives so intensely is because perfect love casts out fear (1 Jn. 4:18). When your sense of purpose and passion is driven by your love for the Creator and His purposes, and you have realized your gift is in operation, something greater than your intellect takes over. Then your emotions cease to hinder your desire for progress. That kind of passion will cause you to seek out every and any means necessary to accomplish your goals. You become fearless. This is when faith is at its best. Fear *cannot* operate when and where faith is in control.

Knowing God loves us so much that He would offer up His Son on our behalf, that He cannot fail, and that He will not let us fail, love becomes the foundation of all we say and do. God's love works in and through us until we walk by faith and not by sight. Remember, "For it is God which worketh in you both to will and to do of his good pleasure" (Phil. 2:13).

3

MERCY: THE EXTENSION OF LOVE

I believe that one of the most misunderstood tenets of our faith is mercy and the function it serves. It is often overlooked when we speak of the wages of sin. I value this opportunity to expound upon this vital issue.

When the children of Israel were delivered from Egypt, we get a vibrant picture of the Passover they would later be commanded to celebrate. Their celebration would not only serve as reminder of their deliverance from the generational bondage of Egypt but also as a prophetic symbol of a greater deliverance that would come in the person of the Messiah. The deliverance from Egypt was predicated on their obedience to applying the blood of a lamb upon the doorposts the night the destroyer was to pass through Egypt to slay the firstborn sons of the Egyptians. The Lord was very specific in His instructions about the age of the lamb, the time of its slaughter, and so forth. Following these instructions insured the Israelites safety and posterity, and guaranteed their passage to the covenant promise of their own land that God made with Abraham. The "blood of the lamb" was the key.

Once they passed through the Red Sea (which typified the lamb's blood but also prophetically referred to the blood of Messiah), they were led into the wilderness to learn of the God of their salvation. While in this learning process, they were given a worship center called the tabernacle. The tabernacle was of a very precise design. The Lord instructed His servant Moses to construct it according to the "pattern" he was shown in the mount. The "pattern" was a revelation of the Messiah, among other things, given to them as a living demonstration of the true and living God and His love for humanity. It was filled with elaborate furnishings that were set in order to tell of the Messiah and God's plan for the ages. From the door to the ark in the Most Holy Place, each piece bore great significance. What I need to focus on for this cause is the brazen altar. This is the place where the anointing of blood was ratified and where flesh died. In this place, sin was acknowledged and covered before the progression toward holier things could be achieved.

THE DIFFERENCE

This covering for sin was insufficient to totally appease the wrath of God. However, it was adequate to provide enough grace for the priest to typify that which was to come in the Messiah. To complete this type, the high priest was required to appear once a year to present an offering for the entire nation. This was known as Yom

Kippur. This offering, a commandment to Israel, was not the first time that God had ordained its use. The word *kippur* or *kippura*, which means "to cover," is used after the fall when God replaced Adam and Eve's fig leaf coverings with the coats of animal skins. This covering was merely a type of what was to come in Christ Jesus: the innocent blood of an animal was shed to provide for the guilt of humankind's sin. Therefore, this kippur would remain insufficient until another type of offering was established by the Messiah.

This all-sufficient offering would be known as an *asham*, which means "sin offering." This asham is encrypted in the Hebrew word for heaven, *hashamaim*. This is significant because it indicates where our true atonement comes from. Christ is the asham. The kippur could only temporarily pacify the wrath of the almighty God. The asham ultimately satisfied the cost of sin's wages. Remember that the kippur is a covering over of sin, while the asham is the instrument of remission. Remission is the taking away of sin. Christ has paid the full price for the redemption of humankind as the asham.

While the tabernacle served the purpose of worship and providing atonement, that grace could only serve the needs of Israel from year to year. The ultimate sacrifice would be made by Christ on the cross. Only this would avail mercy and provide grace for the world. As it is written, "For God so loved the world, that he gave his only begotten Son, that whosoever believeth in him should not perish, but have everlasting life."

THE EXAMPLE AND THE CONNECTION

One of the most important pictures of mercy at work takes place when the children of Israel finally make it to the border of Canaan (Num. 13 and 14). God instructs Moses to appoint twelve elders of the tribes to go spy out the land and see that it is as He said it would be: plentiful and fruitful. Then they could see what they had only heard about to this point: the promise of God for His covenant people. Please allow me to interject that obedience to God will provide revelation of what He has already prepared for you.

Upon the elders' return, they brought back evidence of the fruitfulness of their "promised land." Yet, ten of them yielded an evil (faithless) report. Despite all that God had provided for them during their journey, *they refused to believe* that God would bring them into what He brought them to. Even in light of the admonition of Caleb, *they refused to believe* the evidence they held in their hands and the God who had wrought such a great deliverance.

Remember, they had the kippur, or covering of their sins, in the wilderness that typified what was to come. This helps us to understand what follows their refusal to move forward and possess their promise. God's anger was kindled against the children of Israel. He declared to His apostle Moses that He would smite them with pestilence, disinherit them, and make a greater nation from the seed of Moses (Num. 14:12). Moses then interceded on their behalf and reminded God of His longsuffering and *great mercy* (verse 18). The Lord pardoned the children of Israel but did not allow that generation to pass over into their promise. He gave the promise to their children.

When Moses put God in remembrance of His great mercy, I'm sure He couldn't but help acknowledge the asham that would fulfill His promise. You see, the kippur typified the asham. The covering was to remind them that one day the remission would take place. God's plan was a settled issue and mercy was a key component. The mercy of God allowed them not to receive the consequence of their rebellion. Yes, that generation did perish in the wilderness, but their posterity was preserved because of the mercy of God.

THE RECONCILIATION OF MERCY

Our perception and understanding of mercy are crucial to how we function in our relationship to God and how we communicate the truth of the gospel. When we reconcile an issue, we look to establish that what we end up with is consistent with what we began with. In other words, reconciliation balances the issue at hand. Because mercy involves the shedding of blood and is vital for *atonement* (which shall be discussed in a later chapter), we would profit by looking at why God chose blood for mercy.

The first Adam, before his displacement from the garden, was displayed by reason of typology, to show the creation of the bride. God caused him to be put into a deep sleep, which typifies death. Then He made an incision, known in the Hebrew as a *basor hamul*. It is a circular cut significant of the shedding of blood in man's circumcision and covenant with God. Through this incision, He removed a bone and formed Adam's bride. Then He closed the incision and resurrected the man. This demonstrated in the first Adam that which would be fulfilled in the last Adam (Christ). It would be helpful to know that the most literal translation of Adam's name means "God's blood." God sent His only begotten Son (Jn. 3:16) to shed blood to redeem His first created son

(Lk. 3:38). In doing so, He redeemed the seed of humanity and atoned for all humanity. Please note that the mercy of God redeemed behind the cross as well as beyond the cross. This is proven in the fact that many of the Old Testament saints resurrected and were seen in the streets of Jerusalem after His resurrection (Matt. 27:52–53). As stated in 1 Corinthians 15:22, "For as in Adam all die, even so in Christ shall all be made alive."

Remember that God reconciled all things unto himself in Christ (2 Cor. 5:18). Mercy is a foundational tenet of our faith and undergirds the issue of reconciliation, representing blood for blood and the first redeemed by the last.

To further the point of mercy, we must understand the kinship between God and humankind. The book of Ruth gives a picture of Christ as the *kinsman redeemer*. He marries a Gentile woman, showing the fulfillment that will come in Christ. In that fulfillment, the land that was forfeited was restored. Not only were these things accomplished, but we see a picture of restoration of the old in the new when Naomi nursed Obed. There is a word in the Hebrew: *hadam*. You'll notice that it has Adam's name in it. This word means "pattern." God does nothing without first using a pattern to set the standard for that which He desires to manifest. Therefore, since God is invisible (Col. 1:15), He had to create a pattern to create humans from, and that pattern, or hadam, was Christ. Remember, we are in His image and after His likeness, made to be like Him. That is why only He could serve as our Redeemer. He came to redeem His kin. We are the only things in the order of creation like Him. When He gave us our lives (source), He gave us His essence, which is his Spirit.

Now He takes on a form like His creation to show us what we looked like before humankind's fall and to shed His innocent blood for our sin. That innocent blood had to be presented to the Father, poured out upon the mercy seat in the true tabernacle in heaven to appease the wrath of God finally. When the blood of the sacrifice was poured out on the mercy seat in the tabernacle in the wilderness on Yom Kippur, grace covered the nation for the year to come. Likewise, when the blood (asham) of Messiah was poured out, grace was made available to all who would believe in Christ Jesus by faith. The book of Hebrews gives us this admonition: "Let us therefore come boldly unto the throne of grace, that we may obtain *mercy*, and find grace to help in time of need" (Heb. 4:16; emphasis added). I pray that we embrace how great are the Father's mercies are toward us. In Psalm 136, the psalmist declares twenty-six times that God's mercy endures forever. This revelation of mercy should serve to help us understand just how intense the Father's love is for His children. As flawed as humanity is, the depth of the Father's mercy exceeds the weaknesses of our carnal nature as we grow in grace and in the knowledge of our Lord and Savior Jesus Christ. Yet, without mercy, there is no opportunity to grow. Thank you, heavenly Father for your great and tender mercies. As stated in Romans 12:1, "I beseech you therefore brethren, by the *mercies of God*, that ye present your bodies a living sacrifice, holy, acceptable unto God, which is your reasonable service" (emphasis added).

4

GRACE: GOD'S EMPOWERMENT

> Let us therefore come boldly before the
> throne of *grace,* that we may obtain *mercy,*
> and find *grace* to help in time of need.
> —HEBREWS 4:16 (EMPHASIS ADDED)

*A*s the mercy of almighty God has been appropriated through our Lord Jesus Christ, we now can find our help in the grace of God. As this chapter progresses, I want to look the relationship between mercy and grace, and the function that grace provides for us to mature in the will of God.

I pray that the preceding chapter helped to shine light on the fact that mercy provided covering in the Old Testament, while it remitted sin in the New Testament in Christ pouring out His blood. When this facet of truth is received by the believer, he or she can begin to securely grow and walk in that which grace provides.

The Bible declares, "For by *grace* are ye *saved* through faith; and not that of yourselves: it is the gift of God" (Eph. 2:8; emphasis added). Now, it would be wise for us to first examine the relationship between grace and salvation, or what we think salvation is, so that we may proceed with understanding as we seek to grow in our relationship with the Lord. The word translated *saved* in this passage is the Greek word *sozo* (pronounced sode-zo).

It means "safe," and its applications are to save (i.e., deliver or protect literally or figuratively) and to heal, preserve, do well, be (or make) whole. Hallelujah! What a gift that God has bestowed upon the believer! The salvation of God is so much more that a ticket to a peaceful afterlife.

Let's look further into what is availed to us through the "grace" gift of God. Notice that one of the components of our salvation is deliverance. When we receive the gift of salvation that Christ Jesus provides, we have access to deliverance. Deliverance is deliverance. He does not discriminate. Whatever you need to be delivered from, the Lord has made provision in His Word to accomplish it. The believer must be willing to admit the need is there. Denial ties God's hands, so to speak. One must face what needs to be fixed. Thus, the Lord would ask people, "Will you be made whole?" Just as the Father will not force Himself on anyone, one must understand that there are certain requisites that must be met for the agreement of faith to take place.

Also included is the protection of God. Throughout the Old Testament and especially in the psalms, God declares and demonstrates His desire to protect those He has called unto Himself (refer to Ex. 17:14–16). In the New Testament, he has provided armor for the believer to use on a daily basis. Please be mindful that there are no loopholes by which your adversary can circumvent what God has provided to the believer in Christ through grace. In fact, grace provides such an empowerment that whatever comes your way will be proven inadequate. It cannot stop you from accomplishing that which God has ordained to be done. When the Apostle Paul asked God to move what was troubling him, God reassured him that His grace was sufficient. Paul then concluded that in his personal weakness, the strength of God was made perfect. May we all become so humble to recognize that God that empowers us through His grace to accomplish the works He has prescribed for us regardless of the circumstance.

As we progress through the applications of grace, we come to the provision of healing. One thing our Lord Jesus consistently demonstrated was the Father's will to heal. I believe that most who profess to be saved have overlooked the fact that John records, *"And the Word was made flesh, and dwelt among us, (and we beheld his glory, the glory as of the only begotten of the Father,) full of grace and truth"* (Jn. 1:14; emphasis added). As He was, and is, the Word made flesh, we should understand that the Word still contains healing virtue. God and his Word are one. I am astonished at the modern-day Bible teachers who look to disprove that almighty God still appropriates healing when proper conditions are met. God is the same yesterday, today, and forever (Heb. 13:8). The power of Christ's stripes that healed us (Isa. 53:5) is just as powerful now as when the prophecy was spoken. He still upholds all things by the word of his power (Heb. 1:3), and in Him there is no variableness or shadow of turning (Jam. 1:17). The anointing removes burdens and destroys yokes (Isa. 10:27). The body of Christ is the bearer of the anointing (Acts 1:8 and 10:38).

The next thing that salvation provides through grace is God's ability to preserve. Grace has the ability to keep us from falling (stumbling) and present us faultless (Jude 24). God is well able to keep that which He has committed to Himself. We should understand that it is God who keeps us on the right path, and that we do nothing by our own power. Anyone who has ever wanted to give up or quit while working for the Lord, or even in his or her walk with the Lord, knows that the reason he or she couldn't is because the Holy Ghost provided the strength to continue. The Apostle Paul spoke of a time when he was "pressed out of measure, above strength, insomuch that we despaired even of life" (2 Cor. 1:8). Yet, he didn't give up. He continued onward because of what grace provided.

As we further examine the grace of God, we find His provision of wellness and or prosperity. This issue of prosperity has become controversial even to the point of becoming a stumbling block. Therefore, I pray to bring clarity to the issue of biblical prosperity. I am convicted that scripture provides enough evidence of what God defines as prosperity. As defined in the New Testament, the word for salvation means "to do well" or "to be or make whole." This clearly indicates that prosperity is a holistic matter, not just a financial one. Financial wealth without physical or mental health is not prosperity, and vice versa. Scripture declares, "Beloved, I wish above all things that thou mayest prosper and be in health, even as thy soul prospereth" (3 Jn. 3). This verse helps us to understand that prosperity begins in the soul or inward person and exudes from there. It is a proportionate growth that Father God desires to see in His children and is relevant to His process. Peter writes, "But grow in grace, and in the knowledge of our Lord and Savior Jesus Christ" (2 Pet. 3:18a). Herein is a major point of connection concerning grace and salvation.

Grace was given by Father God through and in Christ Jesus so that the Body could properly reflect or represent Him in the earth. It is His wholeness that we are to seek Him for, not the world's. The world system is satisfied with "misery management" and depravity of all sorts. This is not so in the Kingdom of God. For the believer to settle with anything that Christ Jesus died to conquer, or deliver us from, is to live beneath the privilege of a child of the King. Remember that you are an heir of God and joint heir of Christ (Rom. 8:17). Again, scripture declares, "He that spared not his own Son, but delivered him up for us all, how shall he not with him also freely give us all things?" (Rom. 8:32). We must learn to receive that which grace/salvation provides. Please note I conclude this chapter stating that unbelief will keep anyone out of the "rest" and/or promise(s) of God (Heb. 4:1–6). I pray that the reader will invest the necessary time to investigate the relationship between grace and salvation. The Father will be glorified when you begin to walk out the revelation through the study of scripture.

5
REDEMPTION: GOD'S LEGAL LOOPHOLE

When approaching the subject of redemption, I find wonder and amazement, mostly because of how we define it. To ask anyone his or her most common understanding of the word, one would probably say it is the act, process, or an instance of redeeming. One could simply relate to the root of the word (redeem), which means to buy back or repurchase. For the sake of this discussion, I will amend the definition in *Webster's New Collegiate Dictionary* and state that it also means *to free from what distresses or harms: as to free from captivity by payment or ransom*. This extension of the definition helps us to perceive the love of God in the death, burial, and resurrection of our Lord and Christ. It magnifies John 3:16's statement that "God *so loved* the world" (emphasis added).

When we examine the subject of redemption, we must look at what it accomplished and when it was accomplished. Scripture helps us to understand that the works of God were finished from the foundation of the world (Heb. 4:3). This basically means that God determined everything before He did anything. With that in mind, we can safely conclude that redemption was determined as a safety net (for humans) and a legal loophole (for God) before humans would have the opportunity to sin. Please remember that God is holy! Holiness is the attribute of God by which

He maintains His integrity. Also note that because He is holy, His holiness is the *standard* by which we know sin. It is a standard by which we know sin because we are the only thing in His creation *formed* in His image and after His likeness. We were made for the sole purpose of representing Him in the earth.

I understand that we are spirit first and foremost, and that spirit cannot be seen in a tangible realm, at least not without a host body. What we are to represent is the "character" of God. When that character is compromised, it is known to us as sin. The Hebrew word picture of *sin* is of an archer releasing his arrow but missing the mark. I am belaboring this point so that we may gain understanding of how God views sin and why He has to judge it. Please note, for the sake of clarity, that I said God judges or condemns sin. Yet, we must endeavor to know the relationship between sin and the human soul.

God did not create humankind with a nature to sin, and that was never the intent of God's heart. However, we do come to understand that Adam selected the nature of sin when he elected to exercise his ability to choose "the knowledge of good and evil" over godliness. Remember, according to Genesis 2:16, humans were under the commandment of God. We understand that God gave people the ability to choose (because love must be a choice) but never gave us the right to choose. By this, we know that humans must learn to accept responsibility for our choices and the consequences or rewards thereof. We also must accept that all the depravity humanity has partaken in is a direct result of humans' initial choice to disobey God in the garden. This act of disobedience yielded more than the consequence of being put out of the garden. It wrought a detrimental change in human nature that would become generationally viral.

From this, we should be able to perceive God's judgment against sin. Sin is not an act as much as it is a nature or state of being. Though one can commit an act of sin, the act is because of the nature of sin. The Apostle Paul explained it this way: "Know ye not, that to whom ye yield yourselves servants to obey, his servants ye are to whom ye obey; whether of sin unto death, or of obedience unto righteousness?" (Rom. 6:16).

We come to understand that in the final "judgment," those sentenced to hell will suffer eternal separation and torment because they chose to remain in the sin nature of fallen humankind. Unfortunately, there are many who have chosen this lesser option while attending church and disregarding the Word. This is like the parable of the ten virgins in Matthew 25.

We come back to what redemption accomplished. Since God has always been holy, the wages of sin have always been death. Therefore, foreseeing the possibility of humankind sinning against Him, God predetermined a method by which he could bring humans back into relationship with Him. The method was the virgin-conceived incarnation of the Lord Jesus followed by His death, burial, and resurrection. These were determined and finished before the foundation of the world. This exposes just how great is the Lord's love toward us.

Let's shift lenses and allow this verse of scripture to speak to us about redemption. "For all have sinned and come short of the glory of God; 'Being justified freely by his grace through the *redemption* that is in Christ Jesus" (Rom. 3:23–24). How great is it that our justification is related to our redemption? We are seen as "just" when we approach God in prayer or when we share the witness of Christ with someone. It is a work of His sovereignty and wisdom that has brought us into this relationship. If God says you are "just" in His sight, who dare say otherwise? "Where the word of a king is there is power: and who may say unto him, what doest thou?" (Eccl. 8:4). Why would you believe otherwise? Romans 8:30 reveals to us that our justification with God is the pathway to our ultimate glorification by God. Hallelujah! So great is His love toward us!

Thus far, when we think on what redemption provides by Christ Jesus, we should also be reminded of the forgiveness of sin, being justified with God, and being glorified by God. Redemption also allows for the process of transformation to take place in our lives. Colossians 1:12–14 states,

> Giving thanks unto the Father, which hath made us meet to be partakers of the inheritance of the saints in light: 'Who hath delivered us from the power of darkness, and hath *translated* us into the kingdom of his dear Son: 'In whom we have *redemption* through his blood, even the foregiveness of sins. (emphasis added)

We are translated from the former influence and power of darkness into Christ's Kingdom, in which lies our inheritance. When we look at the term *translated*, we should understand that God has rebuked the darkness that once blinded our minds (2 Cor. 4:3–4) so that we can now move forward into the promise(s) before us (2 Cor. 1:20). It would be beneficial at this point to observe that whatever has a hold on your life, the love of God is greater.

Through your faith in the finished work of the cross of Christ, God commanded the power of darkness to release you. In accordance with the definition in the beginning of the chapter, by the *power* of redemption we have been freed from everything that brings us distress or harm. We must learn how to appropriate these essentials (by faith) to walk in victory in every area of our lives.

As we progress through these tenets, my prayer is that you become more secure in your relationship with almighty God, and understand the depth of His love for all His children. His predetermined will for us is so great and most have chosen to live beneath their covenant privilege. There is a Hebrew proverb I cannot quote verbatim but the essence is on the judgment. We will have to give an account for every blessing we refused to receive. Remember that Jesus said, "'I am come that they might have life, and that they might have it more abundantly'" (Jn. 10:10b). May it please the Lord for His children to look up and live, so much more as we see the day approaching.

6

RECONCILIATION: COVENANT BALANCE

For there to be a covenant, there is usually an equal weight of responsibility on each side. If there are benefits, there are also responsibilities. Yet, this covenant carries a unique dynamic because most covenants or contracts as we know them are between people. This covenant, however, is between God and humankind. What I find most intriguing is that it would seem humankind has very little to offer in such a relationship, yet God saw fit to establish such with us. To proceed in this train of thought, let's examine this issue in the light of its definition. According to *Funk & Wagnalls Desk Dictionary*, to *reconcile* means to bring back to friendship after estrangement; to bring acquiescence, content, or submission; or to make or show to be consistent or congruous or *harmonize* with.

I need to discuss several aspects of this definition to reveal all that God has appropriated for His people through reconciliation. The first is relative to the first definition: to bring back to friendship after estrangement. A clearer picture of the purpose of the gospel of Christ could not be portrayed. Jesus brought his disciples to a point where he told them, "'Henceforth I call you not servants; for the servant knoweth not what his lord doeth: but I have called you friends; *for all things that I have heard of my Father I have made known unto you*'" (Jn. 15:15; emphasis added). In the latter part of this statement, Jesus reveals that He has equipped the disciples with heavenly instruction so they may operate in the earthly realm. We must be cognizant of the relationship between heaven and earth, as we have been instructed concerning our prayer lives (Matt. 6:9–10). We must also be cognizant of the relationship between Father God and His children. Too often, we view Him as a God far away or somewhat estranged from His creation. Remember, we are dealing with reconciliation. Before the cross, there was a sense of estrangement because Christ was still being typified through various offerings. However, since the death, burial, and resurrection of Christ, there is no longer a partition between the Father and His creation except the latter's unbelief. Before I proceed, allow me to clarify a misconception that may be an issue with some. We (humanity) are all His creation, but we *are not* all His children. Without a true confession of faith in Jesus as *Lord* (Rom. 10:9–10) and without being filled with the Holy Ghost (Rom 8:9, 14–16), scripture declares that we are not His. This is where reconciliation becomes most significant. When the creation (humanity) enters into covenant by faith, then the relationship is brought back into friendship.

The next dynamic of reconciliation will require a greater capacity of faith to apprehend. Our Lord and Christ, "who being in the form of God, thought it not robbery to be equal with God" (Phil. 1:6), gives us our best picture of being congruent. This does not mean equal in position, but equal in His image and after His likeness. He rules over everything, and we likewise have been given dominion in the earth. We are to reflect His image in exercising dominion. Remember, we are to conform to the image of Christ (Rom. 8:29), "for in him we live, and move, and have our being" (Acts 17:28). As we further investigate this aspect of reconciliation, we cannot afford to neglect how the Father has reconciled all things unto Himself in Christ Jesus (2 Cor. 5:17–19). This gives us the assurance that we as believers can fulfill the mandates of the kingdom of God.

AS IT IS IN HEAVEN

When Christ Jesus gave us the template for our prayer lives, the secondary focus, after reverence of the Father, was the command for the kingdom's causes and resources to be manifest "on earth as it is in heaven" (Matt. 6:9–10). Through the power of Christ's resurrection, Father God has realigned our ability to fulfill all that He prescribed. That also qualifies the believer to put on the whole armor of God and go forth and witness God's victory made manifest. We should manifest it in our marriages, our children's lives, our finances, and all aspects of our health. One of the main functions of reconciliation is setting things in order to provide victory in Jesus's name.

Yet, it seems many so-called believers in Christ suffer difficulty in reconciling the difference between the world system and the Kingdom of God. The Kingdom of God is a "theocratic order" based on the sovereignty of almighty God. The world system is a multiplicity of governmental structures that may or may not agree. Therefore, conflict is inevitable, whether within a country or between countries. Even here in the United States, states fight against the nation's Constitution and the federal government fights against states to compel them to exercise certain actions, which the federal government determines is its "right." This way of doing things is evidence of confusion and of its author, Satan. "For God is not the author of confusion, but of peace, as in all the churches of the saints" (1 Cor. 14:33). The Word of God provides everything needed in the realm of socialization so we can be spiritually relational to God and one another.

However, in this country, we do not understand the dynamic of a kingdom. What we call a republic employs a democracy that yields it strength to human opinion, which in most cases is the source of self-serving causes. Opinion, which varies from person to person, is the very thing that God warned people not to adopt in the Garden of Eden. What is good? What is evil? Instead of faith and obedience to God's way (the Kingdom), let's figure it out through debate and strife. Let's go to war, literally or figuratively, to see whose opinion prevails. Let's manipulate and scheme behind closed doors with bribes and promises to foster political influence. In these things, humans look to serve their own agenda. That is why politicians rarely do what is truly best for the greater good. They do what they think is best for their own political interests and the interests of those who supply their financing.

The Kingdom, however, is totally inverse in its way of functioning. The sovereign nature of God, at its core, holds to one standard of life and not many. That *standard* is His Word. By and through His Word (the Bible), we comprehend the integrity of God. A true standard is not compromised. For example, if a contractor begins to build a structure using standard American English (SAE) measurements and, in the middle of building, switches to metric without converting, the structure will be unstable, off-center, and unable to withstand atmospheric conditions. Allow me to interject this principle from scripture: "When the enemy shall come in like a flood, the Spirit of the Lord shall lift up a standard against him" (Isa. 59:19b).

If the truth be known, the soul of humankind looks for a standard by which to live but does not realize it is trapped by its opinionated nature. The standard that reconciles all things can only be revealed by the Spirit of God. Again, let us refer to scripture for our understanding. "But the natural man receiveth not the things of the Spirit of God: for they are foolishness unto him: neither can he know them, because they are spiritually discerned" (1 Cor. 2:14). Thus, to comprehend anything relevant to faith requires one to be enlightened by the Holy Spirit. Remember, to seek for the truth of God by any other means is an offense to the standard that God has set.

I pray it has been made clear that reconciliation is God's tool of restoring balance between heaven and earth, Himself and humankind. The revelation that comes with this understanding is that nothing people can do will prevent God's timetable from being fulfilled. The power of that lies in the fact that as one attaches himself or herself to the will of God, his or her destiny shall come to pass. May the understanding of reconciliation bring the balance of God into the life of the reader.

7

RESTORATION: WELCOME BACK

*I*f you have ever seen a car or maybe a piece of antique furniture in its restored state, you noted the glimmer and the shine. Restoration has the ability to highlight the details of the original craftsmanship to the extent that the piece restored becomes like a piece of art—a masterpiece, if you will. Restoration increases the value of a thing over time. In the same light, the restored item regains its purpose (the ability to function according to its original design). This description of a natural process serves to fuel the imagination and foster a spiritual word picture. However, it still falls short of what our Lord and Christ accomplished through His death, burial, and resurrection.

It would be advantageous to look beyond the relational issue He resolved between God and humankind and see the big picture. When scripture declares, "For God so loved the world," the word translated from the Greek Septuagint is the word *kosmos* (kos'-mos). This word is also translated as an "orderly arrangement." It includes the inhabitants of that order as well as the restoration of the moral atmosphere. With this understanding in hand, let's do a mild reconstruction of John 3:16, which states, "For God so loved his (orderly arrangement) that he gave his only begotten Son." This reconstruction should assist us in understanding that the finished work of the cross is comprehensive and exhaustive. Not only have we been restored as His children, but all things that pertain to our advancement in the kingdom are at our disposal. The only hinderance one might experience results from lack of knowledge or personal unbelief. (Refer to Matthew 13:57–58 and Hebrews 4:6).

To proceed into the deeper revelation of *restoration*, we must incorporate the *covenant* that brought it to pass. Often when scripture is discussed or viewed, it is not viewed through the eyes of the covenant. Deuteronomy 7:9 declares that God is faithful and that He *keeps covenant*. Psalm 89:43 declares that He will not break his covenant nor alter that which He has spoken. My reason for laboring this point is to emphasize that when God created, He did so through the vehicle of *covenant*. Please allow me to elaborate about the importance of *covenant* in creation so that a more complete picture of *restoration* may be presented.

The Bible declares that "to every *thing* there is a season, and a time to every purpose under the heaven" (Eccl. 3:1). When the Word speaks of "under the heaven," we must examine the earth, time, and people's relationship to both. Genesis 1:14 reveals that the luminaries of our solar system were placed for *signs* and *seasons* (and for days and years). Please note that chronology is mentioned last. The word *seasons* is from the Hebrew word *moedim*, which means "appointed times."

Fast forward to the establishment of Israel as a nation when they were delivered from Egypt. When Elohim gave them their calendar, He incorporated a total of seven feasts. Each feast bears a significance beyond a chronological cycle. These feasts of the Lord serve as markers in time. They tell the story of Elohim's doings in the earth through the Messiah Yashua (Jn. 1:1–3; Col. 1:13–19). Even as there are seven days in the sequence of creation and seven days in a week, there are also seven (prophetic) days in the economy of the *covenant* God established. Therefore, there is a season *(moedim)* for everything and a time to every purpose coupled with the fact that everything that *God* created was established with purpose (Ps. 33:6, 9; Isa. 14:24–27), which cannot be compromised. It is reasonable to conclude that God created with *covenant* as the forefront and strength of creation. If so, then *covenant* reigns as the "governor" of time. God's purpose in sanctification is in establishing His *covenant* (Gen. 15:13–18; Deut. 8:18). Through the sacrificial death, burial, and resurrection of our Lord Jesus Christ, God not only restored our ability to be in right relationship with Him, but also restored our ability to fulfill his *covenant* purposes in the earth. Now enters faith. God incorporated faith in agreement with His Word to safeguard the integrity of the *covenant*. This is why faith cannot be misused but can be misrepresented and even misunderstood. Since restoration is the topic at hand, we must understand and embrace the idea that faith is the major component in living this facet of truth out in our salvation (Phil. 2:12). This is where the manifestation of the finished work of Christ becomes the "evidence of things not seen."

Restoration also allows us passage into the *promise of rest* that was left to us (Heb. 4:1). The *covenant* that Christ mediates is where all the promises of God are fulfilled (2 Cor. 1:20). Faith in Christ Jesus is assurance in the fact that it is finished (Gen. 2:1–3; Jn. 17:4 and 19:30; Heb. 4:3).

The Apostle Paul prayed for the church at Ephesus to receive the Spirit of "revelation and wisdom" in the knowledge of Christ (Eph. 1:17). Such revelation is essential for the believer in Christ Jesus to understand the dynamics and the mandates of the Kingdom of God. Without said revelation, we fail to comprehend the ways of the Spirit we are supposed to submit to and be instructed by. It also incapacitates the believer from functioning in a state of restoration. In other words, you will never see yourself in the light of who God says you are, and thus fall short of activating your full potential. Restoration brings us back into the truth of "being" in God's image and after His likeness (Acts 17:28).

The restoration from God is beyond human reasoning. God, through Christ Jesus, did more than restore humankind back to a place of relationship (which Adam abandoned). It worked to accomplish something much greater. We never saw the first Adam become what he would have been if had eaten of the right fruit. The Tree of Life was placed in the garden to enhance the man's capability to navigate the greater dimension of the spiritual realm. The man's placement in the Garden of Eden was the only the beginning of his stewardship of/dominion over the earth. He was given life by Elohim, but the Tree of Life would have caused him to have it more abundantly (Jn. 10:10). The inevitability of human obedience would have drawn him closer to the presence of his God and Father.

Enter the last Adam, Christ Jesus, the Lamb of God and our Redeemer. Jesus came to demonstrate to humankind what Elohim had predetermined life to look like. Please note that Jesus came into the earth as a man (Gal. 4:4). However, He was operating by the "anointing" of God (Lk. 4:18; Acts 10:38). Christ has restored us to the original intent of the Father's purpose of our creation, and in doing so has cleared the way for all who believe (by faith) to enter the promise of *His rest*. Embracing this revelation opens the door to untold possibilities. Political, economic, and social climates change when the children of God realize all that we have been afforded. To substantiate this statement, please refer to the following scriptures: Numbers 33:51–56, Deuteronomy 7:16–17, Matthew 28:18–20, Acts 17:6, and Revelation 11:15.

This narrative would be incomplete without noting that not only was the kosmos restored, but also the soul of humankind (Ps. 23:3). Humans have regained the ability to function as the "living souls" they were created to be. Please be mindful the Creator's covenant includes Heaven and Earth. Since humans have been given the responsibility of dominion in and over the earth, we must also partake of that which restoration provided. The soul of a human is the seat of his or her holistic prosperity (3 Jn. 2). Jesus demonstrated that humans were designed to function on a higher plain and understand the laws of operation the greater dimension of the spirit realm as compared to the laws of nature. I am of deep conviction that God never intended for humans to function under the same restrictions as the beasts of the field because they were ordained to have dominion *"over"* them (Gen. 1:26). Allow me to extend my conviction in saying that the laws of nature are as they are because of the fallen nature of humankind and its influence on the environment. Humankind's dominion is to be expressed through the administration of the soul. From there comes the utterance of the spirit (Gen. 2:19; Prov. 18:21; Matt. 12:33–37). The believer in Christ Jesus must take responsibility for the care and condition of his or her atmosphere. The Eden mandate still applies to the commission of humankind. *Dress it and keep it!* To the reader, your ability to exercise dominion has been restored to you. What are you going to do to express the God in you? You are more than a conqueror through Him who loved you (Rom. 8:37). Greater is He that is within you than he that is in the world (1 Jn. 4:4).

The greatest challenge that any believer will face is to move beyond the religious and denominational postulates and predispositions and let the pure unadulterated Word of God have its way. I must state that it would behoove the reader to realistically view the modern history of the church and confess that because of our division and segregationist behavior (in establishing denominations), we have not honored God (Jn. 17:21–22). God is greater than our denominations (of which he ordained none) and that is why He lives outside of them. He cannot be forced to conform to any posture of our will, and He will not conform to our image. Please refer to Psalm 100:1–3. Our gracious Father did not place Christ on the cross for His children to ignore and so they would disobey the mandates of His Kingdom. May we receive the *grace* of God to live out the truth of all the *cross* has provided for us. His Kingdom comes and His will be done on earth as it is in heaven.

8

JUSTIFICATION: DIVINE ALIGNMENT

*J*ustification is defined as, the action of showing something to be right or reasonable. The theological definitions include the action of declaring or making righteous something in the sight of God and the act of God whereby humankind is made or accounted just, or free from guilt or penalty of sin. Allow me to use these verses of scripture as a launching pad.

> For I am not ashamed of the gospel of Christ: for it is the power of God unto salvation to everyone that believeth; to the Jew first, and also to the Greek. For therein is the righteous of God revealed from faith to faith: as it is written, The *just* shall live by faith. (Rom. 1:16–17; emphasis added)

Just as justification works in the processing of a document to bring the text into alignment, it also works with the righteousness of God to do the same for the believer in Christ. The Word of God declares to us that Christ Jesus was made to be sin for us that we might be made the righteousness of God in Him (2 Cor. 5:21). It is the sovereign God's desire that has brought us back into alignment with His love and covenant purpose.

Further examination of the scriptures should encourage your heart to walk in this facet of truth while strengthening your faith. Romans 4:25 explains that the resurrection of Christ was for our justification. How is that for the love of God on display? Again, Romans 5:1 causes me to understand that justification by faith in Christ allows me to inherit the peace of God. When God speaks of peace, it carries more volume than the human mind conceives. Remember that the peace of God passes all understanding, and it guards our hearts and minds through Christ Jesus (Phil. 4:7). Also note that this peace does not exist outside of God Himself, and it cannot be obtained unless He provides it (Jn. 14:27).

When God speaks of peace, it goes much further than the lack of agitation and the presence of calm. This peace embraces a greater sense of security and stability. The word picture presented by the Hebrew word *shalom* is one of a thorny hedge of protection. Within said hedge abides wellness, health, and prosperity. We only access this peace by an unwavering faith in Christ Jesus. I know that it's God's will for us to receive it and abide in it according to Isaiah 26:3.

I believe it advantageous to explore how righteousness serves as the catalyst for the believer to experience justification. The term *righteousness* is said to mean being in right relationship or right standing with someone (i.e., God). It can also be found in legal documents, in reference to being in alignment with a particular statute or law. We should view ourselves in the light of this truth. God has sovereignly brought us back into alignment at the good pleasure of His will (Eph. 1:5). Because of your righteousness, you have been justified with God, and He has justified your use of faith to accomplish His will. When I say the believer is justified to use faith, bear in mind that faith is the supernatural element of God that reveals God and His intention. Since we are His righteousness, we have assurance and confidence that He will support or endorse His word and its proper application and operation (synchronization with times and seasons).

To further the aforementioned point, the use of faith is set only to establish God's purposes in the earth. The entire purpose for the creation of earth is to manifest God's desire for His Kingdom (Matt. 6:10). It is my personal conviction that the purpose of faith has been incompletely communicated and thus our ability to perform the will of God has been diluted and limited. Covenant is at the heart of all God has done, as affirmed by Jesus's words, "'It is finished'" (Jn. 19:30).

Let's examine scripture to gain insight into God's desire to establish His Kingdom. The prophet Isaiah provides powerful insight into the salvation the Messiah would accomplish. Chapter 9 verse 7 lets us know that the Messiah is coming to (re)establish His government in the earth.

> Of the increase of his government and peace there shall be no end, upon the throne of David, and upon his kingdom, to order it, and to establish it with judgement and justice from henceforth even for ever. The zeal of the Lord of hosts will perform this.

Since the time of humankind's displacement from the garden, the atmosphere of earth and the social dynamic of humankind has been corrupt. Physical, emotional, psychological, and social maladies have become common place. The masses have become numb to the depravity that continuously corrupts the moral and ethical fiber of our society. *The government of people cannot rectify the problems it is responsible for creating.* Only God can provide, and has provided, the answer to restructuring our world and introducing humankind to true peace. Therefore, Christ Jesus came to give us God's plan to realign humankind with its creator. Every statute and judgment set forth in the Word of God is to assure equitable living and fairness in recompense and to aid in creating generational legacies for all. Observe the heart of God for His people in these verses: Exodus 23:27–30, Numbers 33:55, and Deuteronomy 7:17.

Although these are Old Testament references, they exhibit covenant purpose. The covenant serves the same purpose as light, which is to displace darkness. God desires to see His people as a light to the nations as they establish His covenant in the earth (Deut. 4:5–8 and 8:18).

In light of this, justification reigns strong. The statutes of the Kingdom of God keep its citizens in harmony with one another and in *alignment* with God. Remember that is what justification does: it brings things into alignment. Your faith has brought you into alignment with God and His plan of salvation, which is greater than your personal passage to eternal life. Your justification has ushered in a dynamic of God's will that has global implications. That means your life is more relevant than your everyday routine and the way you see yourself. The God of your faith has provided you with gifts and abilities that bring you into a greater framework of life and speak to your destiny. You are responsible for exercising your faith as a righteous ambassador of the Kingdom of God. Angel armies await to hear the voice of His Word proceed out of your mouth (Ps. 103:20; Heb. 1:14). Jesus has provided a "blood bought, covenant right" for the believer to exercise his or her *birthright* as a child of the Most High God (Rom. 8:16–17). You have a reservoir of resources at your disposal (Js. 5:16b; 1 Pet. 1:4) waiting for you to use it for its Kingdom assignment. Remember,

God is not just the source; He is the inexhaustible source. The Kingdom of God has never been subject to economic recession or depletion of any kind and never will. God does not ration His resources; He appoints and designates, just as He did when He called you into the Kingdom (Jn. 15:16; Col. 1:13).

In my closing admonition concerning our justification, I implore you the reader, the believer, to activate your gifts that God's grace has provided through faith. Live your faith out loud. Carry yourself according to what God has provided, and how He has positioned you in His Kingdom. You are more than a conqueror through Him who loved us (Rom. 8:37). You are complete in Him, the head of all principality and power (Col. 2:10). I cannot overemphasize the importance of understanding that when Christ Jesus shed his holy blood on the cross and suffered death on behalf of those who would believe in Him, He provided a complete and great salvation (Heb. 2:3). Everything the believer would need is included. The Father did not spare and deliver your soul and empower you by His grace to leave you destitute and lacking (Ps. 23:1). You have been justified by your faith in the Son of the Most High God. Live like it!

9

ATONEMENT: THE ULTIMATE CONNECTION

I am under the sincere conviction that the word *atonement*, as it relates to the believer, is understood best in the phonetic breakdown: at-one-ment. This awesome act of the Father's will has brought the believer in to a *position* of oneness with the sovereign King eternal. Believers must understand that atonement is incorporated into the prayer of Christ in John 17:22–24. Now the believer must accept the reality of being positionally aligned with God (Jn. 14:3; Eph. 2:5–6) and assume the responsibility thereof. Responsibility is an understated element of the believer's position in the covenant. One of the main truths overlooked in the relationship that Elohim established is that there is a responsibility on the behalf of the believer. God fulfilled His self-imposed responsibility in the death, burial, and resurrection of Christ Jesus. Through this, we understand that all that is needed for our faith to be exercised is in place and complete or, should I say "finished." Believers cannot realistically expect the transforming power of faith in Christ to serve merely as a mental assent to a group of facts, while the cloud of witnesses provides so much more evidence. In order to experience covenant benefits (Ps. 103:2), one must adhere to covenant responsibilities (Deut. 28:1–2). One might struggle with these Old Testament references, but it is wise observe that the principle of covenant remains the same whether old or new.

Atonement is the all-encompassing element of the covenant by which we experience the grace of almighty God. Israel was commanded to observe the Day of Atonement, *Yom Kippur*. *Kippur* means "to cover." It was a temporary appeasement of the wrath of God. We move through the timeline of God to the crucifixion of Our Lord Christ Jesus, where the "true atonement" takes place. The Bible declares that "but now once in the end of the world (age) hath he appeared to put away sins by the sacrifice of himself" (Heb. 9:26b). The difference is that while the blood of bulls and goats could only serve as a temporary substitute to cover the sins of the Israel, Christ became the Lamb of God that took away the sins of the world (Jn. 1:29). Again, allow me to mention that in the Hebrew tongue is the word *asham* (a-sham), pronounced with the short *a* sound. This Hebrew word is contained within another word: *hashamyim*, the word for heaven. The revelation is that our sin offering (the perfect atonement for the souls of people) was provided out of heaven by God Himself (Gen. 22:8). This translates to Christ being our "Passover Lamb" (1 Cor. 5:7). Our atonement means that Christ became the propitiation for all sin for all people. His redemption reached behind the cross and redeemed Adam, then went forward and waited for you and me.

Indulge me as I expound a bit further concerning the awesome love of God that has spawned this wonderful truth. All the souls of people have been atoned for. Yet, the issue of salvation by grace is dependent upon whether or not an individual receives this gift of salvation by faith. I perceive that the common perception of the Greek word *agape* is somewhat distorted. Yes, it is true that God's display of love was not dependent upon any merit on humanity's part (Rom. 5:8), but it is contingent upon "whosoever believes on him" (Jn. 3:16). To reject the gift, in essence, is to reject the giver. It is also to be in denial of the truth and integrity of God's being and the need we have for the gift of salvation because of the human condition.

In order to become "faith functional," one has to submit to his or her need for divine absolution. Since the sin offering is provided by God, it stands to reason that people cannot atone for themselves. The proof of the human condition is evident by the widespread depravities that plague or world. "Humanity is one!" No matter where on God's earth we travel, we will find similar social ills. Countries fortify against one another when their resources could be better utilized collectively. Differences in social and spiritual philosophies will not allow our world leaders to aid each other for the cause of the greater good. Rather, they cower in fear of one another because they see others as they see themselves: with secret agendas fueled by the need for power and dominance. (As an interesting footnote, we were created to have dominion over the earth, as stated in Genesis 1:26–28, not over each other.) The generations of people were to function under the same divine mandate no matter where they migrated to.

> And God blessed them, and God said unto them, be fruitful, and multiply, and replenish the earth, and subdue it, and have dominion over *the fish of the sea*, and over *the fowl of the air*, and over every living thing that moveth upon the earth. (Gen. 1:28; emphasis added)

The reason the I emphasized the fish and fowl is to bring clarity to the point that there are those among humanity who misplace the order of God as it relates to His creation. In doing so, they overemphasize the place of animal life in making animals equal to themselves. Yes, we do have a responsibility as the governors of the earth to properly steward all natural resources. However, God did not make animals in His image and after His likeness, which disqualifies any sense of equality between man and beast. To substantiate God's viewpoint, let's allow the voice of scripture to be our point of reference.

> For the invisible things of him from the creation of the world are clearly seen, being understood by the things that are made, even his eternal power and Godhead; so that they are without excuse: Because that, when they knew God, they glorified him not as God, neither were thankful; *but became vain in their imaginations*, and their foolish heart was darkened. Professing themselves to be wise, they became fools, And changed the glory of the uncorruptible God into an image made like to corruptible man, and to birds, and fourfooted beasts, and creeping things. (Rom. 1:20–23; emphasis added)

When examining the issue of atonement, it becomes clear that humankind, who is the pinnacle of God's creation, could only be atoned for by the Creator (Ps. 100:3). The beauty of this truth stems from the fact that just as the high priest had to make an atonement for himself on Yom Kippur, our Great High Priest made an atonement for Himself. He made Himself the offering for us who are made in *His image and likeness.* This may be difficult to understand and perceive, but when Christ redeemed and atoned for humankind, He redeemed and atoned for His image.

This is a facet of truth that makes our salvation so great (Heb. 2:3) and our God even greater (Ps. 96:4 and 145:3). Please embrace the truth of scripture that declares the heart and mind of God when He said, "Let us make man in our image, after our likeness, and let them have dominion" (Gen. 1:26a). *You are God's image in the earth!* That statement screams of "atonement."

Your soul, your very being, is eternally bonded to the image of God. Why else would He take the form of humanity and serve our greatest need, allowing for the reposturing of our hearts in righteousness? The being of humankind is so precious to God that in our atonement, he ingrafts us unto Himself (Acts. 17:28; Eph. 1:4–5). You get it! We are a part of Him! Our being is His essence (Gen. 2:7). To deny this truth is to deny His love for you (Jn. 3:16). This forces you to live in the torment of uncertainty while being made subject to the temporal impositions of a deceitful world system.

I respectfully submit that all the data one may have collected while yet unregenerated, whether intellectual, emotional, or spiritual, only serves to prevent one from obtaining the truth of God. According to scripture, the mind of unbelief is blinded by the adversary so the glorious light of the gospel cannot shine through.

We were once enemies of God and the cross (Rom. 5:10; Phil. 3:18) having enmity toward God (Rom. 8:7). Yet, this undeniable display of love we call atonement beckons us to reason that our value to God cannot be equated with anything. We are priceless. Again, the scripture declares,

> Forasmuch as ye know that ye were not redeemed with corruptible (*perishable*) things, as silver and gold, from your vain conversation (*aimless conduct*) received by tradition from your fathers; But with the *precious blood of Christ,* as of a lamb without blemish and without spot; Who verily was foreordained before the foundation of the world but was manifest in these last times *for you*. (1 Pet. 1:18–20; emphasis added)

Atonement avails us of heaven's resources (Js. 5:16) and the Father's benefits (Ps.103:2) to the extent that He has purposed to make himself known to all (Matt. 28:19–20; 2 Pet. 3:9).

In my closing admonition concerning this matter, I sincerely implore you to investigate the depths of God's love and desire for you, as He sees you. Gain His perspective.

Ask yourself if there was another way (an easier way) to accomplish the atonement of humanity that didn't require the sacrifice of leaving His throne and assuming the likeness of a man (Phil. 2:6–8); being tempted in all points, as we are (Matt. 4:1–11; Heb. 4:15); and suffering betrayal and death at the hands of those He came to redeem and atone for. Don't you perceive that He would have done it? He didn't atone through the vehicle of the cross to show off. He did it because there was no other way, *"for God so loved."* I pray that you will avail yourself of the opportunity the Father calls all of His children to experience. This is not a church thing. This is a kingdom mandate. Remember that you, as a born-again believer in Christ, are an ambassador of His Kingdom (2 Cor. 5:20). It requires a resolve and a tenacity to fulfill the words of our Lord and Christ: "And from the days of John the Baptist until now the kingdom of heaven suffereth violence, and the violent take it by force" (Matt. 11:12). Put on the whole armor of God and let's get to it!

10
ALL THINGS WORK TOGETHER

> And we know that all things work together
> for good to them that love God, to them who
> are the called according to his purpose.
> —ROMANS 8:28

There is a popular train of thought commonly accepted surrounding this verse of scripture that incorporates life's situations and circumstances. The idea is that whatever circumstance and/or situation arises, the believer in Christ will reap some type of benefit to move him or her forward in the purposes of God. In addition, the positive things one experiences somehow neutralize all adversity. While I don't disagree that there are lessons to be learned in some of the human experience, and some that can be inspirational, I must differ from that vein of thought. Our everyday environment is in a fallen state and some things were not ordained by God to occur. To believe that God used some form of evil or malfeasance to test and grow our faith is contrary to scripture (Js. 1:13–15). While considering that God is more than able to comfort us in our times of despair and pain (2 Cor. 1:3–5), we must understand that things such as divorce, murder, and the like do not factor into *advancing* anyone's walk of faith.

Second, the believer in Christ should base his or her growth and progress on the things that God has provided for us to flourish (Ps. 1:1–3; Matt. 7:24–27; Phil. 4:8). Whenever a believer incorporates fiction with faith, it creates leaven and becomes toxic to the soul. It leaves the mind trying to filter out what is of God and what is not. In essence, the carnal nature is inadvertently employed, and one is left to distinguish between the fruit of good and evil.

It is imperative for the believer to focus on the Lord (Isa. 26:3) and His provision (Phil. 4:19) to fully embrace the value of the foundational scripture. What has God provided to work in a collaborative effort for the good of His children? Remember, our victory is against things adverse to the purpose of God's Kingdom. As I examine the surrounding content of the collective text, I find the empowerment of God working together for the good of the believer.

Outlined in the preceding chapters were essential tenets of our faith accomplished by the crucifixion, burial, and resurrection of our Lord Jesus. Everything begins with who God is: "love" (1 Jn. 4:8). By the sequence just mentioned, we understand that love is an action. It is not a feeling, but a state of being that finds its motivation in a commitment to compassion and to advancing one's purpose and destiny. To go a step further, "God so loved" because God is love. Everything He does is a result of who He is. God is love, so He does love; God is merciful, so He gives mercy; God is gracious, so He gives grace, and so on. Because He is love, He determined to give of Himself to the benefit of His creation.

The next facet to enter the equation is mercy. His mercy endures forever (Ps. 136:1–9) and endures to all generations (Ps. 100:5). He is great in mercy (Ps. 145:8), therefore He is also slow to anger. Mercy is the attribute of God that allows Him to see what He created, instead of what we've made ourselves into. The remittance of sin that mercy provides is so powerful that I would be remiss not to display an Old Testament truth on how mercy and righteousness work together. When Israel refused to cross over into their promised land, as recorded in Numbers 14, the Lord's anger was greatly kindled against them (verses 11–12). They were spared destruction by the intercession of Moses, who typified Christ seated at the right hand of the Father making intercession for the saints (Heb. 7:25). Note, this intercession could not be made without blood upon the mercy seat. To validate the point in Numbers, beginning in chapter 22 and culminating in chapter 24, the prophet Balaam, who King Balak hired to curse Israel, speaks an interesting word. Instead of a curse, we hear these words: "He hath not beheld iniquity in Jacob, neither hath he seen perverseness in Israel: the Lord his God is with him, and the shout of a King is among them" (Num.

23:21). Was not this the same God that asked Moses to step aside while he smote the Israelites and disinherited them just a short time before? The mercy of God displayed their righteousness (right standing). I'd say that is a strong example of the elements of faith working together for those who are called according to His purpose. Even though their lack of faith closed the window on that generation, He would not allow any curse, from an outside source, to impede their destiny. Remember, whatever God has purposed carries generational impact.

I aspire to conclude with the tenet of grace. As in the chapter on the subject, I clearly stated it is the empowerment of God. The testimony of the Apostle Paul desiring to be delivered from the agitation of the adversary is a clear illustration of how grace conquers adversity. Under further review of that text, one should find that it not only provided the courage to press forward, but also served to resolve some inward issues (2 Cor. 12:8–10). Also, please refer to 2 Corinthians 1:3–10. Remember that by definition, a few of its applications are to heal, preserve, and do well and be or make whole. Grace is encompassing as it relates to meeting the needs of the believer.

We are to walk as ambassadors in establishing the Kingdom. The power of prophecy is why God equipped you with faith. The next time you read Romans 8:28, remember the context of the chapter. In doing so, know there is "therefore now no condemnation to them which are in Christ Jesus, who walk not after the *flesh*, but after the *Spirit*" (emphasis added). Then, look into the Spirit and remember what almighty God has supplied: love, mercy, grace, redemption, reconciliation, restoration, justification, and atonement. They never stop working together for your good.

Afterword

Faith holds the key to the mind of God. Every step of faith taken is designed not only to move us forward in God's economy and on His timeline, but is also profitable in revealing a dimension of wisdom, understanding, and power that enhances our ability to function in the spirit realm. No one can function or operate in or above the revelation of Christ he or she does not possess. Please note that Jesus stated in John 14:6, "I am the way, *the truth*, and the life" (emphasis added). I highlighted the word *truth* to express that truth is manifold or multifaceted. I put it in the perspective of a prism. A prism is designed to show the composite nature of light. When held up to the light, we are able to see that light has a deeper consistency than in our limited perception. The prism reveals what the naked eye cannot see: that light is multifaceted. Likewise is our Savior, Christ Jesus. We require the revelation provided by the Word of God to operate in the fulness of His stature.

Any revelation missing or disregarded allows for breach, by which a fiery dart of the wicked can be launched from the gates of hell. Christ has covered all bases so we are complete and lack nothing (Acts. 17:28; Col. 2:10–15).

Faith protects the integrity of the covenant. No one can access the inheritance of the saints, which the covenant provides, without faith. Too many believers in Christ Jesus fail to access the inheritance that faith provides because they do not obey what they hear (Rom. 10:16–17; Js. 1:22–24). We must not only embrace the reality of our inheritance as a part of our birthright, but also note that God does not take it from us (1 Pet. 1:3–4); we choose to forfeit it (Matt. 25:14–29). No Kingdom resource shall be wasted. Too often, we forget that our God is the epitome of *benevolence*. Because He makes it rain on the unjust as well as the just (who live by faith), we confuse what is good with what is God. Besides, who gets to decide or define what is good in the life of the believer? Being bought with a price such as the blood of Christ—is that not God's prerogative? Can you really discern a good thing fostered by the world's entrapment from a God thing that comes by reason of *inheritance* (Prov. 10:22)? Dependency upon the world system with all its entrapments has veiled the reality of our true dependency upon almighty God. The world system (and its fallen atmosphere) is designed to veil unbelieving minds (2 Cor. 4:3--4). One can believe in Christ for salvation or even deliverance for a particular area in life. Yet, that does not mean that he or she believes in Him for every area of his or her life (Mk. 9:24). Do not make the mistake of confusing what you think is good (by the world's standard) with what God has *provided* us by and through His Spirit.

While a majority of people profess to have faith of some sort, the plurality of Christendom cannot properly relate to the fullness of what Christ accomplished through His death, burial, and resurrection. We are provided throughout the Word with many examples of faith at work, but the Bible only offers *one* description of faith (Heb. 11:1). What is it about the modern-day western hemisphere religious machine that will allow us to read the same book and remain comfortably divided? This has been a puzzle from ages past. This book is written with the aspiration of changing the focus of the born-again believer. *The Substance of Faith* is written to provide a sound biblical perspective of the foundation God laid in Christ Jesus (Matt. 7:24–27; 1 Cor. 3:11). No one can properly administer faith without comprehending its substance at the foundational level. Jesus stated, "'He that is not with me is against me; and he that gathereth not with me scattereth abroad'" (Matt. 12:30). This book is written to

| 99

transcend denominational lines and religious arguments and present a scriptural platform of unity. Its base lies in Ephesians 4:3–6. Even though we cannot dwell under the same roof, we *can* be of the same mind (1 Cor. 1:10). May this book provide practical application concerning that which we need to please God: *faith*!

Printed in the USA
CPSIA information can be obtained
at www.ICGtesting.com
CBHW071958291124
18173CB00045B/838